SECOND EDITION

Media Queens | Crown & Compass Life
(crownandcompasslifecoaching.com)

Editor And Chief: Nicole Easton
Creative Content and Marketing Editor: Julie Drost Lokun
For Inquiries On This Publication Contact- 847-361-9518

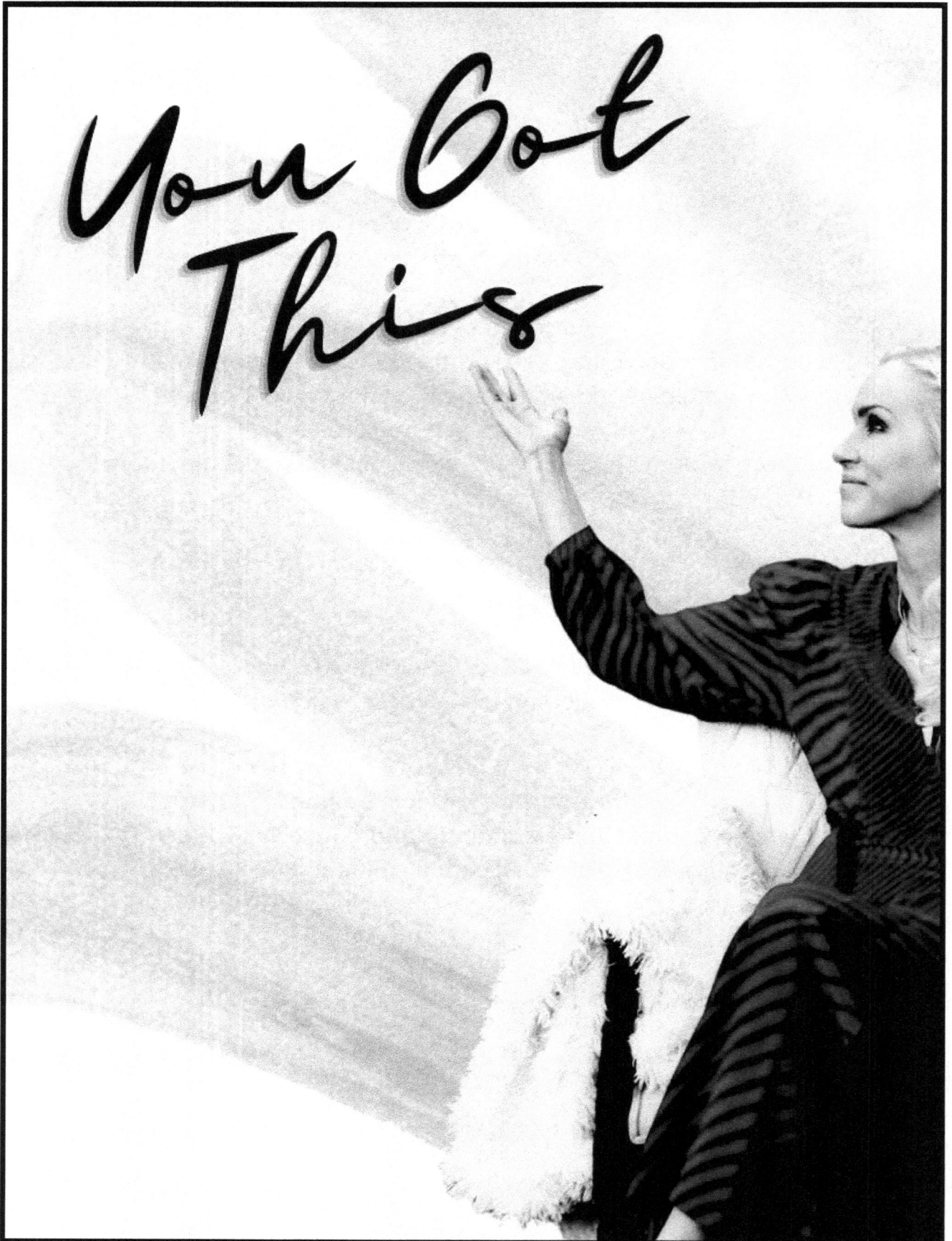

You Got This

CONTENTS

> **"ALL YOU NEED IS 20 SECONDS OF UNBRIDLED COURAGE TO DO SOMETHING MAGNIFICENT."**
>
> *Julie Lokun, Author, Boy Mama, Wife & Facilitator of Dreams*

↓ <u>DEDICATION</u>

STOP CHASING YOUR DREAMS & START BEING

Dedicated to my family, whose belief in me inspired me to Hustle Smarter.

<u>My Mother</u>-Who always told me I could do anything and believed in me even when I stumbled.

<u>My Father</u>-Who led by example, an entrepreneur who made his dream a reality.

<u>My Husband-</u>Who allowed me the space to be creative and quirky and reinforced that I was on the path I was meant to be on.

<u>My Kids</u>-All four of my beautiful boys, whose curiosity and unabashed excitement reminds me of what is truly important.

HUSTLE SMART©
Stop Chasing & Start Being.

DEFINING THE HUSTLE SMART ENTREPRENEUR

He/She is a visionary that leads with a mission. The HSE takes chances, seizes opportunities, and is a lifelong learner. The HSE does not quit their day job to launch their new business. The HSE strategically hustles while maintaining a consistent flow of income. The HSE squashes inner-doubt and laughs at the imposter syndrome. The HSE is unabashedly authentic and navigates their business with integrity. The HSE is resilient and learns from the fumbles along the way. And the HSE has an innate intelligence and hustles the smart way.

Hustle Smart is a term I coined and use with my clients as bold verbiage to elicit their dream of capturing the abundance of life's riches.

Hustle Smart is a resource to navigate that entrepreneurial whisper.

Hustle Smart is the belief that using this method; you can take your idea and make it a thriving business.

Hustle Smart is how I took my idea and made it into a thriving business in less than one year.

Now I share this method with you. This guide book will teach you how to be an entrepreneur who possesses enduring persistence. You will hustle with an innovative brain. You will hustle my way, the smart way.

LET THE HUSTLE BEGIN.

LETTER FROM COACH JULES

"Collect Experiences, Not Riches." - **Julie Lokun**

Dear Reader,

Even as a small girl, I was colored as a passionate, free-spirit. Family historians commented on my ability to embrace extraordinary opportunities. While meandering through various electrifying experiences over the years, I was met by an eclectic group of mentors who lit my soul on fire. These moments and people opened my heart to unique opportunities and quieted the bubbling murmurs of self-limiting thoughts.

As a girl, I looked at sparkly new ventures as a chance to meet new people and learn new things. I never factored "failure" or "what- ifs" into the equation. I understand that most people are not wired this way. I recognize that grounded, forward-focused people typically take an approach anchored with a well-thought-out blueprint. My gypsy-like navigation coupled with my "I can do anything" attitude met with stumbling blocks. However, these obstacles were not walls of resistance for me. They were the pages where I learned the most valuable lessons.

During my entrepreneurial exploration, sometimes I soared, and other times I plummeted. What has been constant in this entrepreneurial equation was my ability to get back up after setbacks, brush off my boots, and learn the lessons of my journey.

My fumbles along this path are now the teaching tools I impart to clients. Using a steady cadence of trial and error, I have created a functional roadmap that offers others the opportunity to revolutionize their ideas and ultimately monetize their service or product.

My personal story began with a spark. I had just finished my Master's Certification in Life Coaching, and I wanted to practice this craft on a bigger scale. I recognized that coaching was my calling. Coaching was my Ikigai.

Coaching is my Ikigai

What is "IKIGAI"? Ikigai is a Japanese concept that means "a reason for being." The word refers to having a direction or purpose in life that makes one's life worthwhile

This mission, or Ikigai, is a primal calling from within, and I knew I was destined to live my life as a coach and lead the coaching industry with an authentic and innovative practice.

This entrepreneurial drive was sparked by a lightning bolt. The revelation hit me—I was an ENTREPRENEUR in the making. I needed to take this idea and make it a real, thriving business.

I approached this business idea with my usual Figure-it-out-as-I-go-style. Spending countless hours basking in the dimly lit glow of my computer, I educated myself on launching a coaching business online.

Google became my teacher as I learned how to distinguish myself from the multitudes of other coaches that crowded the world wide web. Podcasts became my touchstone as I drank the Kool-Aid of the hustlers who went before me.

I dove deep into Facebook and Instagram to understand algorithms and the advertising cycle. I experimented with different forms of social media. And I made mistakes. One error was that I concluded that **Pinterest** was an out-of-date platform and that it reaped little benefits. I failed to realize that Pinterest is a search engine (not a social media platform) that can be as powerful as **Google**.

My path of educating myself landed in the bowels of **YouTube.** I also taught myself how to edit and make videos. With scrappy determination, I am proud to say I became a novice website designer. Perhaps my most satisfying accolade was when I taught myself how to create and market an online mastermind group. This became an extension of my practice and now boasts a nation-wide community of like-minded growth-seekers who meet weekly. The list of accomplishments I am proud of is lengthy.

To say that I was obsessed is an understatement. I spent days upon days lapping up every tip and trick to take my business to entrepreneurial prodigiousness. Through plucky ingenuity and a genuine belief in my skill set, my mission-based idea grew into a life-giving, full-time business in less than a year.

Does this sound impossible?

I guarantee that making your entrepreneurial dreams come true is possible. If your idea is born out of love and if your quest is purpose-driven and not money-driven, you have the best chance to succeed. The bottom line is that because I was able to launch my coaching business successfully, I am doing what I am most passionate about—imparting wisdom and guiding people toward living the life they were meant to live.

YOU GOT THIS- *Coach Jules*

GETTING STARTED

You Have A Gift. You Have A Great Idea. What's next?

I always ask myself, "why not" instead of "why."

This is a learned skill strengthened by trial and error. I wanted my legacy to be more than a woman with a passel of diplomas and a professional acumen of decent jobs. I knew my purpose was to change the course of people's lives, but I didn't know how to go about it. I was plagued with self-doubt, insecurities and often played into the stereotype of the dumb blonde. These self-limiting beliefs were easy for me to fall back on until the discomfort of being mediocre outweighed the discomfort of my fear.

I implore you to take a look at the big picture. Take a look at the overarching vision of your life and ask yourself—*Am I actively pursuing my dreams?* Or are you languishing in self-doubt? If the answer is the latter, actively settling for what-is, try to articulate where and when someone told you that you were not worthy of an abundant life. Who told you that you were not worthy of living a big life? These voices from the past can be voices that originated from your self-doubt, a parent, or a teacher. Once you recognize these negative loops of self-talk, you can pause. Then, you repeat these messages and replace them with a new voice that shouts, "YES, I CAN"!

OPTIMIZE YOUR HUSTLE!

ASSESS YOUR ENTREPRENEURIAL SKILL SET AND MINDSET

As you explore the idea of taking your idea to the next level, it is important to assess your commitment and drive. Do you have the attitude of an entrepreneur?

First, let's explore the four pillars of the optimal entrepreneurial attitude.

DRIVE, DETERMINATION, AMBITION, INTELLIGENCE

This is the time to reflect.

→ Do you have a great idea?

→Do you have the grit to ride the wave of volatility?

→Are you flexible in thought yet steady in your approach to lead when times are lean?

*Exercise: Start with these questions and journal your response below.

- What is your gift or idea that you want to monetize?
- Do you have the aptitude to see this idea to fruition?
- Do you have the mental space to open yourself to new ideas and innovation?

_____

_____

_____

_____

_____

"Don't worry about being successful but work toward being significant, and the success will naturally follow." **-Oprah Winfrey**

What Is Intelligence?

- Aptitude To Gather Interpret and Prioritize Information
- Commercial Intellect
- Motivation
- Ability to scan business environments
- Ability to discern weaknesses, threats, opportunities, and trends.
- Confidence and courage to be decisive and assured (not cocky)
- Curiosity

*Exercise: Hustler Smart Ask

Be honest with yourself. What do you need to work on, and how can you work on your entrepreneurial intelligence?

_____

_____

_____

_____

_____

Reality Check

Hustle with a <u>Mission-Based</u> Mind-Set
Not A <u>Money-Based</u> Mindset

I am convinced that when you create a business simply to make money, you are setting yourself up for disappointment. When your idea isn't layered in a true passion or purpose, your clients will feel the disconnect. Your strength will falter in times of fiscal decline, and quite often, this will lead to burnout. When your venture is based in purpose, the energy you devote to creating a viable business is tapped from a well of dedicated momentum.

⚵ IMPLEMENTATION OF YOUR HUSTLE

While assessing your skills in regards to launching your product or service, ask yourself this:

Do you have the:

- Communication aptitude for expressing yourself, your mission, and your idea clearly and concisely?
- Motivation to work extra hours, to go that extra mile to make your idea a mainstay in your audience's mind?
- Self-Discipline to devote your energy to making your idea work?
- Persuasive leadership to direct your prospective audience and elicit the importance of your idea?
- Speed and Agility to get things done?

*Exercise: Which of these skills do I possess? Which could I improve upon?

_____

_____

_____

_____

THE IMPORTANCE OF RESILIENCY

A Hustler has "the capacity to recover quickly from difficulties; toughness."

Resiliency is an essential component of structuring your idea and making it a reality. Often the road to fruition is laden with messy moments. With resilience, you can bounce back from failure and learn from the most important lesson an entrepreneur can encounter.

*Exercise: Hustlers Thought Download

Do you have thick skin? How do you deal with failure?

_____

_____

_____

_____

_____

_____

As an entrepreneur myself, I have encountered situations that could have deterred me from my original mission. I have dealt with self-doubt, imposter syndrome, staffing issues, time management—just to name a few. I stayed true to my overarching vision of my business and looked forward to rethinking my approach.

The HUSTLERS HARD ASK

*Exercise: Do you have a business-driven mission? And if so, what is it?

_____

_____

_____

_____

_____

How can you shift your business mission from being money-driven to purpose-driven?

_____

_____

_____

_____

_____

MISSION STATEMENTS

Take time to craft a mission statement. What is a mission statement? A mission statement, whether personal or professional, encapsulates the driving force behind your idea. This is essential to remind you of your overall mission and to unite your future team. A personal mission statement is designed to help you set goals that will drive change in your life; to do that, you must first understand what drives you. These are called your principles and values. These principles and values are fundamental truths about ourselves; they are the fabric of who we are, whether we are consciously aware of them or not.

Coach Jules Mission Statement: To be a teacher, that educates and empowers my clients to optimize their human potential.

*Exercise: Mission Statement. Craft your Mission Statement below:

_____

_____

If you are having a hard time putting your mission statement into words, use my go-to guided exercise to prompt your mission statement with ease.

This is my go-to online tool that sparks creativity.

→ https://msb.franklincovey.com/

*Exercise: **Postscript:** After completing this exercise, tuck your mission statement away for a few days and circle back to the draft. How do you feel about your statement? What points still resonate? How can you condense this statement into a bite-size message?

_____

HOW YOUR FEARS CAN DETRACT FROM YOUR SUCCESS

→ AGE

→ LACK OF FINANCES

→ FEAR OF REJECTION

→ LACK OF EDUCATION

*Exercise: OVERCOMING YOUR NEGATIVE MINDSETOnce you have admitted it, you can control the fear of the unknown.

Write a list of your fears in regards to launching your business.

1.

2.

3.

4.

5.

Are these fears based in reality, or are they perceived fears of what may or may not happen?

1.

2.

3.

4.

5.

Of your original five fears, which ones can you cross off your list because they are not reality-based?

_____

_____

_____

HUSTLE UNTIL YOUR HATERS ASK IF YOU ARE HIRING

You have taken the time to understand your idea. You have a solid understanding of the grit and strength it takes to Hustle Smart.

Now it is time to put your idea to action.

"Never confuse motion with action." **-Benjamin Franklin**

SWOT ANALYSIS

Analyze your business idea with this tool. Look at projected strengths, weaknesses, opportunities, and threats. Use this tool quarterly as you progress in your business venture. It will help you assess your positioning and bring clarity to future projections.

Hustler's Tip: This is a great habit to practice quarterly.

Example of A Quarterly SWOT Analysis

Hustle Smart

SWOT ANALYSIS

Strengths

Weaknesses

Opportunities

Threats

YOUR NEXT STEPS

You have what it takes, the idea, the grit, and determination. You now have a clear understanding that there is the potential to monetize this business. And you know that businesses that are merely focused on the bottom line or making a quick buck end up as soul-sucking voids in an entrepreneurial venture.

DRUM ROLL PLEASE...

You are now at the intersection in your journey, where you must begin planning. Planning and research are essential in positioning yourself as a thought leader or expert in your industry. Without a comprehensive analysis of the market, your likelihood of success is diminished. Lack of Research is the reason why so many start-ups fail.

Let's Talk About Research

Types of research:

- Market Research
- Trends
- Cost Overhead
- Marketing (Positioning)

The ones
who are crazy
enough to
think they
can change
the world,
are the ones
who do.

STEVE JOBS

The Hustler's Business Plan

*Exercise: Overview: This Business Plan will be the foundation of your professional mindset. Read and recite this daily.

My mission and purpose are to:

_____

_____

_____

My business is evolving into... (a team of... based in...) Be as detailed as possible :

_____

_____

_____

To achieve my business vision, I will:

Three-month Goal:

_____

_____

Six-month Goal:

_____

_____

Twelve-month Goal:

_____

_____

I am grateful I am able to solve this problem for my clientele:

_____

_____

My service or product allows my clients to:

_____

_____

Without my help, my clients will:

_____

_____

_____

As I focus on my work, I gain clarity that my services will better my clients' lives.

The most important action steps I need to take daily are:

#1:

_____

#2:

_____

#3:

_____

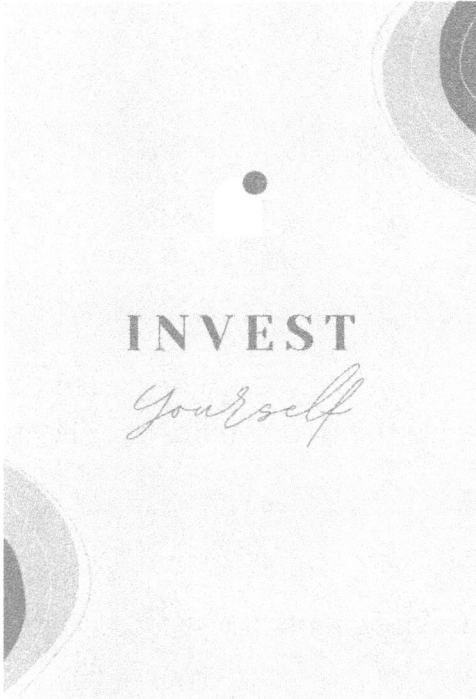

SECRETS TO SUCCESS

Here are a few tips to strengthen your entrepreneurial endeavors that have worked for me. You are not an island. Reach out to those who have done this before you. Their wisdom will be invaluable.

Get a mentor-A mentor in your field can be the secret weapon that elevates your business to the next level. Preferably find a mentor that is a few steps ahead of you in your entrepreneurial journey so they can provide you with their wisdom. Mentors often have a deep understanding of what works and what doesn't work and will guide and support your trajectory.

Tip→You can sign up for free mentor matching at **www.score.org**. This is an invaluable resource that provides a mentor in a similar industry.

Understand Proximity-It is essential to create proximity to the industry you wish to position yourself in. For example, if you are a photographer, join networking groups, talk to other photographers, and offer up your expertise for free. The most important thing is to meet people.

Avoid Failure at All Costs

BIGGEST REASONS FOR ENTREPRENEURIAL FAILS

INADEQUATE PLANNING
UNDERESTIMATING THE COMMITMENT
CASH FLOW
POOR MANAGEMENT
STAFFING ISSUES
MARKETING
PRICING RESEARCH
LACK OF COMPETITIVE EDGE
GOING IT ALONE
GROWTH TOO FAST

BRANDING

Branding is the essential element in creating a connection with your audience.

A Brand Can Be Anything

We are used to thinking about brands in relationship to companies and products—Think McDonald's or Apple. But nowadays, anything can be a brand. Even as an individual, you have a personal brand.

So what is your personal brand? Whether you're known for your snaps, or you're still using a typewriter, you have a brand that exists both on and offline.

Luckily, there are many great tools and resources to help you with the personal branding process. Use them to leave the right impression on people who look you up online.

The idea of personal/professional branding makes some people uncomfortable. But, if you don't take control of your personal brand online, you are missing out on opportunities and letting others control your narrative.

While the specific circumstances and goals vary by entrepreneur, the overall concepts and process are still applicable to every entrepreneur.

PERSONAL BRANDING

And why this matters

"Without a story, you are just an inanimate object. A story elicits a connection that brings you and your vision alive"- **Julie Lokun**

It just so happens that personal branding is an obsession of mine. Often, I get the obligatory eye roll when I present the question, "What is your personal brand"? I am met with responses such as, "I don't need personal branding" or "This is an uncomfortable space. It seems so narcissistic". The truth of the matter is that if you don't control your brand, others will. You are creating a personal brand just by existing. People make judgments based on how you present yourself.

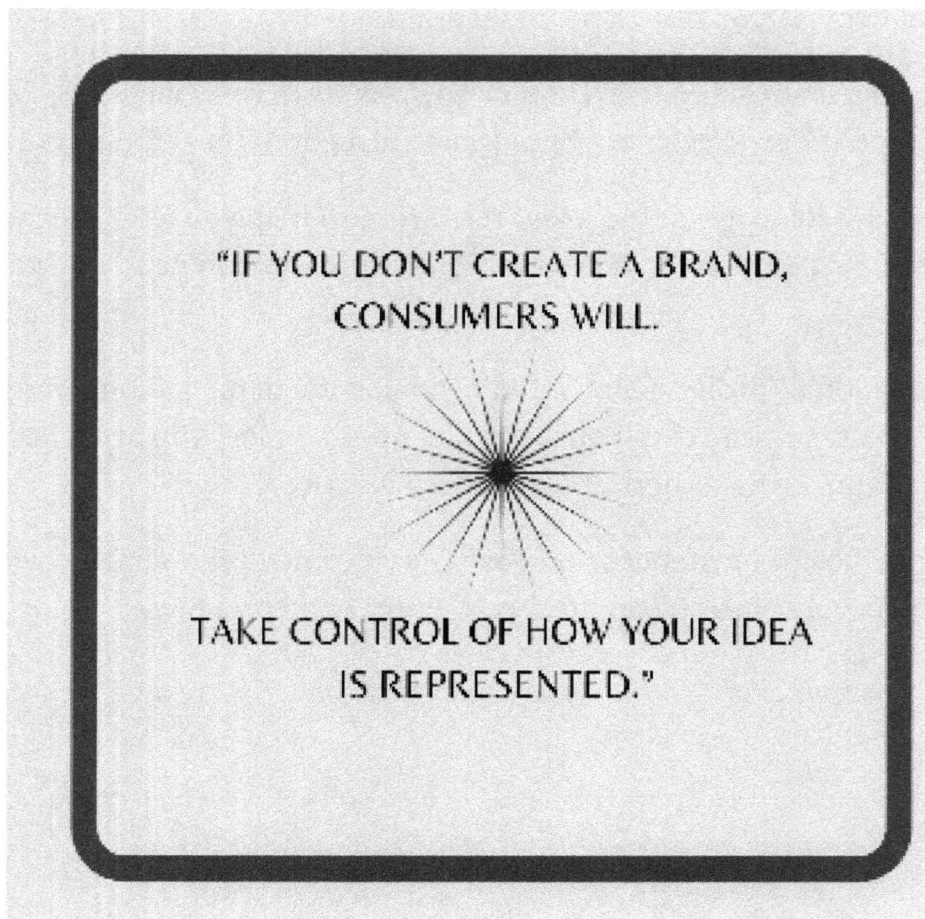

"IF YOU DON'T CREATE A BRAND, CONSUMERS WILL.

TAKE CONTROL OF HOW YOUR IDEA IS REPRESENTED."

Personal branding is an essential cog of the professional branding machine. This simply means a personal brand is the essence of who you are as an entrepreneur. By embracing your brand, you live this brand intrinsically and extrinsically. Your core values and beliefs are directly reflected in how you present and manage your professional identity. So, personal branding and professional branding are one and the same.

To further clarify, branding is an illustrative description of what you, as a human, represent. Do you represent integrity? Are you creative? Maybe you have a bohemian heart? The list is endless.

*Exercise: Take a minute to pause and write down Three cornerstone phrases that represent you.

1.

2.

3.

Analyze these key phrases and articulate how they distinguish you in a personal and professional realm.

_____

_____

_____

_____

_____

_____

_____

YOUR BRANDING STORY

Sharing a story with your audience is key in connecting with any demographic. Anecdotes personalize the experience and garner trust and loyalty.

*__Exercise:__ What is your story? What led you to this point? How has your product or service played a pivotal role in making your life better?

_____

_____

_____

_____

_____

_____

_____

How Can You Incorporate Your Story Into Your Branding or Marketing?

_____

_____

_____

_____

_____

_____

MY BRANDING STORY

When I decided to launch my coaching program online, I knew I wanted to distinguish myself amongst the multitude of other coaches that inhabit the online space. Let's face it; life coaches are a dime a dozen. Not to diminish the coaching profession, as we figuratively have locked arms to uplift our fellow humans. But, quite honestly, this unregulated industry allows every Tom, Dick, and Mary to hang a sign on their door and magically transform themselves into a coach. I knew I was different. I knew I brought to the table a legacy of advocacy and a pedigree of higher education that set me apart from the rest. Screaming these hard facts to the world was simply not enough.

Know Your Audience

Understand the problem you will solve for this collective group of potential clients/customers.

I started my branding journey by focusing on my potential client and adding significant value to their lives. I grabbed a nubby number 2 pencil and scratch paper and started to brainstorm. Who do I connect with in my life? Who do I, with casual ease, attract to my circle? I knew, fairly quickly, that I had the ability to foster profound relationships with women and teenage girls. (I apologize to Jeff, Larry, Josh, and the handful of evolved guys that "get" me). But in all sincerity, I knew my superpower was connecting with women and raising their vibrational energies.

I also had a clear vision of how I could add value to their lives by redirecting their patterns and creating a space where they could elevate their self-esteem. I also recognized I could distinguish myself as a coach because I offered a background in journalism and law. My strength is my educational foundation, and I relished with unabashed glee when potential clients were surprised by these degrees in law, journalism, and life coaching.

What distinguishes my brand is my ability to foster an authentic connection with my clientele and instill real tools to elevate their careers, relationships, and overall wellness.

★ I help my clients remove their proverbial tarnished crown from atop their heads. I assist them as they polish it and reposition it, so it shines for all to see.

↓

★ MY BRAND, Crown & Compass, elicits the feeling of how I facilitate client's dreams by anointing and pointing them towards a life of peak performance.

↓

So-> I <u>ANOINT</u> them with confidence and <u>POINT</u> them in the right direction.

↓

= MY BRAND: ANOINT + POINT | CROWN & COMPASS COACHING

⚓

YOUR TURN: Hustler's Brainstorm

*<u>Exercise</u>: Articulate three words that conceptualize your personal values. These are values that you present simultaneously in your personal and professional life.

i.e., passionate, empathetic, and creative.

1.

2.

3.

How can you elicit these three Core Concepts to an audience?

_____

_____

⚘ <u>MARKETING</u>

Hustle Smart Guide To Creating an Online Presence and Audience-Targeted Marketing

The demand for an online presence is non-negotiable in launching your business. If you are a staunch objector to Facebook, Instagram, Pinterest, and similar platforms, I urge you to reconsider. Taking time to understand the power of social media engagement is a necessary evil when unleashing your brand onto the world.

<u>Hustler's Tips:</u>

- Try Googling Yourself. What pops up? Your future client will very likely Google you to understand your reputation. What do you want your clients to see?
- Attaching your "brand" to Social Media Platforms will help you get "seen" on Google. Because Facebook and the like are a powerful presence on Google, having social media accounts will boost your rankings on Google and other search engines.

Prior to establishing a foothold on these social media platforms and launching a marketing campaign, you will need to have a cohesive "look" that is an extension of your brand's message.

<u>More Tips:</u>

- Use the same filter for all your photos
- Keep the photos simple
- Include people in your photographs. Photos of People=More Interest
- If you are taking photos by yourself, use portrait mode on your phone
- Hire a novice or a friend with a good camera to take pictures of you
- Have a plan. Sketch out your ideas for your photos and ensure that your product/service is adequately represented
- Hire a professional photographer
- Be creative and have fun

(Tips Continued)

- Use natural lighting
- Create a story
- Create a call-to-action
- Barter with photographers
- Use Stock Photos (Unsplash, Pixabay)

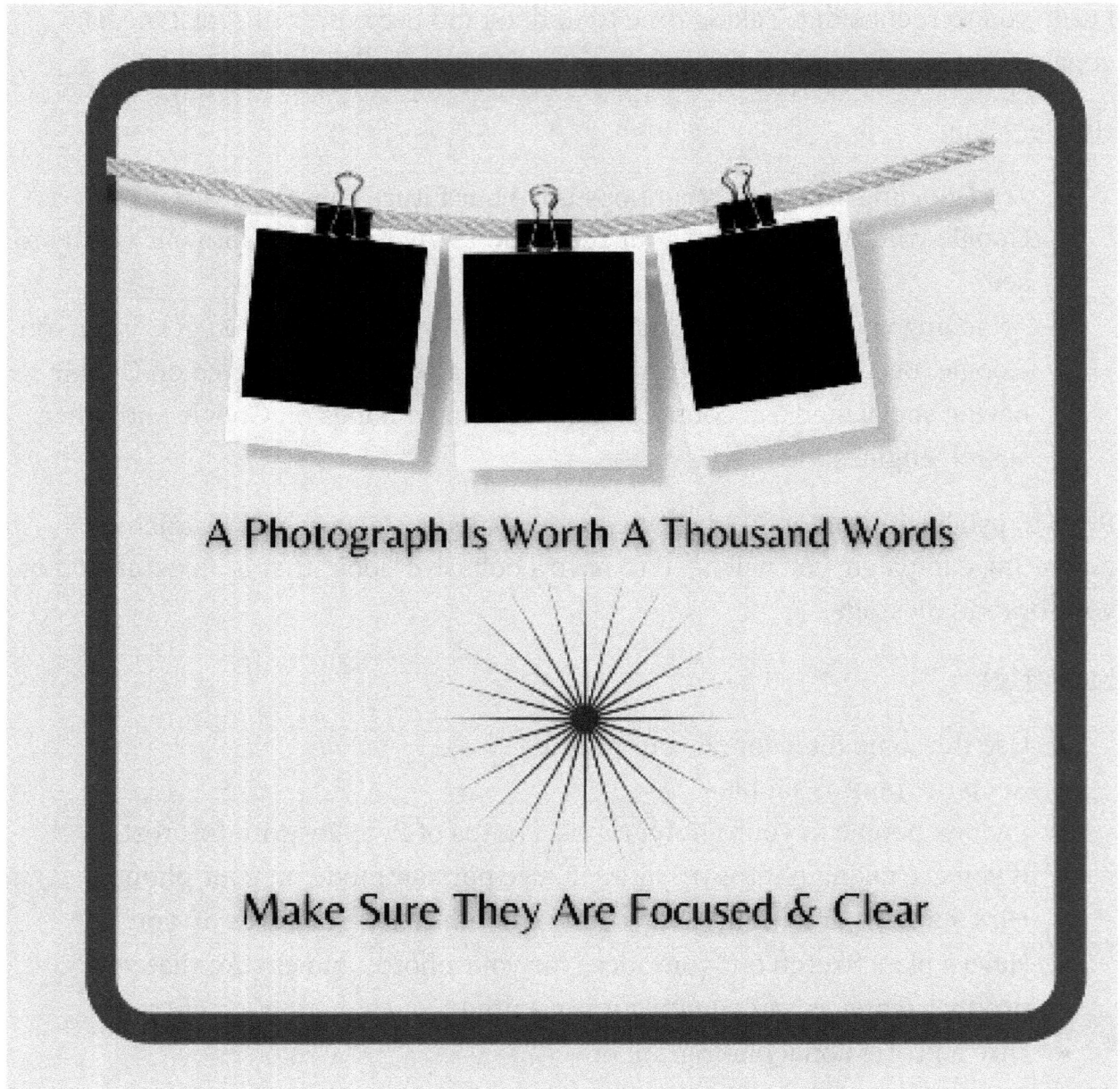

A Photograph Is Worth A Thousand Words

Make Sure They Are Focused & Clear

Vehicles to Propel and Market Your Online Presence

★ Facebook Business
★ Facebook Lives
★ Email List
★ Your Reputation
★ Instagram
★ Instagram Live
★ Pinterest
★ Press Releases
★ Podcasts (court podcasts to be a guest)
★ Community Involvement
★ Networking
★ A website (WordPress, Wix, or Shopify)
★ Google Business
★ Google Ads
★ YouTube Channel
★ Partnerships With Other Companies
★ Media (features on your service/ product)
★ SEO Management (Search Engine Optimization)
★ Etsy Shop
★ Ebay
★ Online Course Creation
★ Blogging
★ TikTok

The marketing journey is complex and ever-evolving. I offer free in-depth Hustle Smart marketing webinars to explain how to utilize these marketing tools. This list is a skimmable summary of powerful vehicles to gain visibility. I will revisit this concept later.

FINANCING YOUR HUSTLE

This is where the real meat of your business begins or ends. How much are you going to need to finance your business? Where will these funds come from? Practice forecasting possible costs. This chart will provide a framework for estimating future expenditures.

Profit and Loss Forecast					
	Month	Month	Month	Month	Month
Sales Revenue					
Variable costs					
Gross Profit					
Fixed Costs					
Rent					
Labor					
Utilities					
Phone					
Insurance					
Advertising					
Accounting					
Miscellaneous					
Total Fixed Costs					
Net Profit (Loss)					

Ways to Fund Your Business Venture:

→ Crowdfunding
→ Family
→ Venture Capitalists
→ Angel Investors
→ Grants
→ Loan
→ Personal Savings

If you are looking outside of yourself for start-up capital, you will need to put together a polished pitch for your investors.

Find the Right Investor-For a lot of founders, a pitch starts the moment you shake hands with an investor. Confidence in yourself and your idea will create an atmosphere attractive to potential investors.

Prepare Your Pitch Deck-Once you've found the right investor, it's time to start preparing. Create a short yet powerful presentation. Get your investors excited about your idea. (Think **Shark Tank)**

Tell Your Story-The point of a pitch is to inspire and excite, not put people to sleep. A personal anecdote woven into your pitch helps you make a connection with investors.

Nail Down the Details-Arguably, the most important thing you can do in a pitch meeting is to talk about the nuts and bolts of your operation. Do your research. Understand net profits. Explain marketing strategies. The bottom line is that your audience will want to understand their return on their investment.

Explain How You Will Solve The Problem-Clearly detail how you are uniquely qualified to solve the problem your potential clients face.

THE IMPORTANCE OF MAKING YOUR BUSINESS LEGAL

1. **Always Use Written Contracts-**(Avoid Oral Contracts) I have heard this question before, "Is an oral contract enforceable?" Yes, it is, but try to prove an oral contract in court! It is always best to CYA or Cover Your Ass. Even if it is an email or pieces of paper, you need to get everything down in writing. Have a "meeting of the minds" documented, so your project isn't sabotaged by someone's selective memory. Again, even an email between parties detailing what you both agreed to is better than nothing!

2. **Properly Categorize Workers-**(Independent Contractors Vs. Employees) Properly categorize your workers. There is a common misconception that business owners don't have to pay taxes on independent contractors. In reality, if you have a contractor acting as an employee, then they are an EMPLOYEE. The law will come down on you hard if you miscategorize a worker. It makes sense to do it the right way from the start and to avoid problems. I have seen several companies go out of business because they miscategorized workers. With the help of an opportunistic attorney, disgruntled workers won a Labor Board hearing, which classified the workers as employees and awarded missed mealtime and overtime pay. If you haven't been paying your workers properly, you have to pay penalties. Additionally, you may have to pay legal fees to defend against the lawsuit you will probably lose. A simple, inexpensive way to protect yourself from an employee lawsuit is by putting together a well-written and **comprehensive employee handbook.**

3. **Register Domain Names For Your Business-** (Names that Identify Your Business Brand) Register a few domain names that contain the name of the brand that you are trying to build. There is nothing worse than building a brand and finding out that a cyber squatter has bought your name and plans to extort you for a large amount of money before he or she turns it over. Be proactive. Register and maintain those domain names early. Try **www.godaddy.com or www.wix.com.**

4. **Register Your Trademark-**A trademark is the legal basis of any brand. It is the logo or the name associated with the product or service you are offering. Registering your trademark protects you from having no recourse if someone uses a similar mark for the same product or service without your permission. Initially, safeguarding your brand may not be a big concern, but the point of all your work is to one day be successful and build a brand. When that happens, then there will be people coming out of the woodwork trying to associate themselves with your brand. Also, note that there is a way that you can reserve your trademark while you are building your brand. That is a pretty smart way to start because, initially, you may not have the evidence needed to secure a trademark registration.

5. **Create an Entity-**The number one legal step you should consider when setting up a new business is creating an entity. That means forming a limited liability company (LLC) or incorporating (forming a corporation) for your business. The main reason for this is that you want to keep things separate. ALWAYS keep your personal assets separate from your business assets. Imagine someone sues you for a business matter, and they end up winning a judgment against your business and you personally. They could collect from your personal assets, like your bank accounts, home, car, etc. It's one thing to lose business assets in a lawsuit, but it's much more devastating if you lose personal assets. That could affect your personal and family life. You don't want a judgment holder from a business lawsuit to be able to collect from your personal assets, and vice versa. Check out **Legal Zoom**. This is a fast and easy way to create an LLC for your business.

6. **Business Insurance-**My parents believed in over-insuring to prevent future problems. So, I would be remiss in not mentioning that a well-oiled business plan includes insuring yourself against potential lawsuits.

You Got This

So Now What?

The Hustler's Legendary Launch

You have a firm foundation on which to build a thriving business. You have clarity in terms of what your business will look like, and you are confident in your ability to deliver a service or product that will most likely change the world. So now what? How will you attract paying clients who will pay for the commodity that you offer?

Many voices flood the internet, telling you how to land the sale. If you Google topics on marketing, your screen will flood with other businesses trying to make the sale. The overwhelming information contains marketing funnels, marketing campaigns, and similar calls to action that infuse brand awareness. These tools have their place. However, if these funnels and campaigns all worked, everyone would be a millionaire.

What Works?

There is no formulaic equation that can concretely predict monetary abundance. The time-tested approach begins with making a connection with future customers and rewriting their stories. This may sound vague or like gibberish, but we tell ourselves stories all day long. We tell ourselves that we need a particular beauty product or that we need to strive to be the CEO of a specific company. These stories tell us what we think we need and want. They can be stopped in their tracks when your powerful connection alters how a customer thinks about his or her story.

When potential clients understand that their story includes your product or service, they rewrite their experience, and the neuroplasticity of their brain changes.

First, understand your audience. Research to understand where this demographic spends most of their time. Are they on Instagram, or are they driving on a freeway daily, passing a display of billboards that often catches their eye? Once you have ascertained clarity about where your audience spends most of their time, you will then embark on the first pillar of building your business. The first step in connecting with this demographic is to build visibility.

> ## The Four Pillars Of Business Building
>
> ### VISIBILITY
>
> ### ENGAGEMENT
>
> ### LEADS
>
> ### SALE

THE FOUR PILLARS OF BUILDING YOUR BUSINESS

VISIBILITY

ENGAGEMENT

LEADS

SALE

I will focus primarily on the first pillar, visibility. Visibility is the cornerstone of making your brand a powerful presence, which ultimately leads to closing the deal. Visibility is where you build a reputation and relay protocol about how your service or product is an agent for change.

Visibility is where the muscle of your hustle flex. It draws upon a consistent flow of quality content and your ability to tap into a deep reservoir of resilience. Without visibility, you will not get the leads that materialize into a sale.

Visibility is everything.

If you start with the *land-a-sale mindset*, you ceremoniously extinguish the foundational element that creates a long-lasting, economy proof brand that will leave a stamp on your professional legacy.

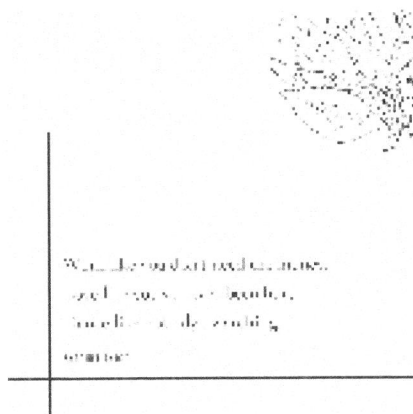

The Hustle Smart Secret Sauce

Harnessing the Power Of Visibility

Once you have a clear understanding of where your audience spends most of their time, you can get the creative juices flowing and reach your audience in unexpected ways. You can reach people through different avenues without the intention of making a sale. Instead, you will extend your brand presence by affiliating yourself in proximity to people that may connect with your vision.

Experts say that your audience needs six to twelve experiences seeing your name, product, or service to remember it exists. This can be an overwhelming thought. However, when you do it strategically, the cadence of your brand identity will start to seep into the DNA of those who need it the most.

Where Do You Begin?

So Many Ideas. So Much Opportunity. The good news is that there are many avenues you can utilize to start spreading the gospel of your fabulous new business. What is even better is that it doesn't have to be a huge financial investment. Although, I do believe in the old adage, "It takes money to make money." You can create a swirl of interest by using creativity and good, old-fashioned elbow grease.

Here is my go-to list that I use for my personal business and, in return, share with my clients.

Website- Do not even think of launching without a website. Building a website that reflects your brand is the cornerstone of your business' visibility. Without a solid website, you will lose credibility and potential clients. This doesn't mean you have to spend thousands of dollars on a larger than life platform. It means that your brand needs to hold space on the internet as a reference for your customers. This is something you can do on your own or hire a professional. I am a self-taught web designer that explored various hosting sites until I got it right. My go-to website builder is **Wix**. It is user friendly and has a large variety of templates that you can choose from. If you are selling products, **Shopify** is a wonderful tool to display and sell your products. Other popular platforms are **Square Site, WordPress,** and **GoDaddy**. And if the mere mention of building your own website has you quaking in your boots, hire out a designer. Freelance designers flood sites like **Fiverr** and **Upwork.** Simply list your requirements and budget, and you will have experts knocking on your door. Find a designer who understands your vision, has excellent references, and has the time to walk you through the design process.

Other things to consider:

Affiliations-Partner with similar businesses and team up with them to promote similar visions. This will exponentially increase the audience of both ventures.

Swag-This is a critical yet straightforward cog in connecting with clients. It can be as simple as a business card or as elaborate as customized samples to give to your clients, pre-sale. It endears customers to your brand and is a reminder that they can't live without your service or product. Customized merch creates a brand presence and doesn't have to cost a fortune. My go-to favorite is **www.discountmugs.com.** I have used this site to customize mugs, pens, shirts, and journals. My clients are always giddy with excitement when they receive a personalized gift with a note that expresses my gratitude for their trust in me.

Or check out ALIBABA, an overseas site that delivers bulk items at a discount at **www.alibaba.com**

Free content-Creating visibility simply means sharing your vision. _Free content is an extension of your vision and will create trust and a reputation with your future customers on an intimate level.

What does FREE CONTENT MEAN?

This broad concept can be boiled down to this. It is an idea that allows your potential customer to have a taste of what you offer. Don't hold your ideas so tight that no one is able to have a sample of your delicious product or service. The act of distributing free content sets the stage for establishing your reputation in your industry.

Free Content Can Include:

- **Blogs**
- **Facebook Lives**
- **Videos on YouTube**
- **E-Books**
- **Webinars**
- **Tutorials**
- **1:1 Introductory Session/Meeting**
- **Books**
- **Speaking Engagements**
- **Lunch and Learns**
- **Sample of Product**

Charitable partnerships-I champion every capable human to give their time, services, resources, and expertise to those in need. This philanthropic act should be executed with no intention other than to make the world a better place. The noble act of volunteering does have added side-effects, in that you will be able to make connections, network, and allow people to witness your overall mission.

Contest or Challenge Pre-launch-This is a savvy entrepreneurial move to offer an attention-getting challenge. At the end of the challenge, offer a package or product to the grand-prize winner. Contests drum up unexpected excitement about the new business. It takes time to prepare and execute your pre-launch. However, when you emit extra energy, the enthusiasm is contagious. I offer challenges bi-yearly. Typically, they are five-day personal development challenges, and I swathe the winners in high price-point coaching packages worth nearly one thousand dollars. I don't approach my challenges with the mindset that I will make money due to my efforts. These challenges are launched to strategically expand my visibility and brand.

YouTube Channel-Even if you aren't camera-ready, turn on your smartphone and give YouTube a try. Not only is **YouTube** a platform that garners increased visibility, but the website will also boost your rating on Google. **Google** is the gold standard of search engines. I believe that by harnessing the algorithms of this monolith, you will have clients flocking to your website.

Paid Advertising-Google Ads-Google is an entity unlike any other. Whether you like it or not, it is a necessary evil. Dabble in **Google Ads.** You can pay as little as $3.00 a day to start creating a rhythm of website visitors.

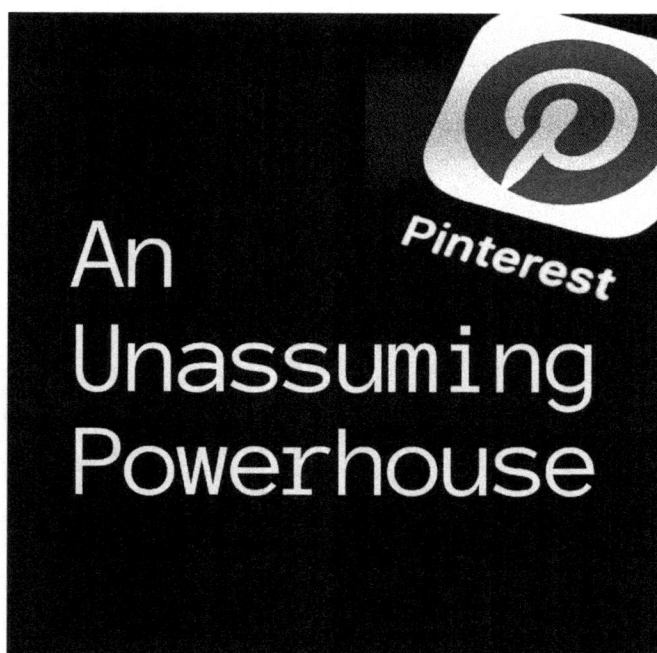

Pinterest-(I'm obsessed with the sleeping giant.) Don't be fooled by this unassuming powerhouse of a search engine. Yes, I said search engine. Many users are misinformed about Pinterest's power, and they often label it "social media." I'm obsessed with this platform since it is a Google in disguise. Pinterest attracts users that are in the discovery phase of a search. Users are looking for recipes, or clothing, and even inspiration in their lives. And, the amazing part of the user experience is that users are poised to purchase. The algorithms are such that content can be used and reused, unlike social media platforms. The Pinterest algorithm soaks up current pins. For example, if it is February, pins that smack of love and Valentine's tend to garner more interest.

How do you start on Pinterest? Use your **Canva** account to create appealing visuals that are not blatant advertisements. First, think about your desired audience and ask yourself, what would this audience be interested in? My desired audience is interested in personal and professional development, so they are most likely drawn to words of inspiration of personal growth tips.

Don't make your pin specific to a sale or advertisement. Draw in your audience with a visually appealing display of something you represent. For example, a client who happens to own a bakery should post a recipe or a photo of a decadent pastry. This will expand visibility.

Remember, visibility is the key to establishing your brand.

Why Pinterest Works-When you draw a client in with your vibrant pin, you have the opportunity to expand on this pin in your content. When a user clicks on the pin, it immediately takes them to your website. This provides a one-step process. A photo and simple content attract a user; then, they are swept to your website, where you can elaborate on your life-altering product or service. The simple 1-click step of getting a user to your website will lead to client engagement and a possible sale. (Remember, simple is better. The more a user is required to navigate different platforms, the more likely you will lose their attention.)

What's even better?

If a Pinterest user pins one of your pins to their board, all of their followers will experience your brand. Pinterest has the capability to expand your visibility exponentially.

→ Hustler's tip: Budget a little money to invest in **Pinterest Ads.** You can budget as little as two dollars a day, and your pins will be seen. My website hits doubled in the first week of testing out this marketing strategy.

*The demographics of Pinterest are 80% women. However, women have untapped buying potential. I typically curate my pins to be female-centric.

Press Release-Sharpen your Number 2 pencil and start writing. Write a short snippet on why your business will change the world. Remember, it must be newsworthy, so craft a vignette of why it is crucial that the community learns of your work. Once all the T's are crossed and the I's are dotted, search local papers, magazines, and media outlets that may be interested in your story. Look for a page on their website that allows for press release submissions. Send your story their way and sit back and wait for your inbox to start clamoring for more! Press Releases are another amazing vehicle to gain visibility and boost your ranking in Google.

Podcast Pitches-Ask yourself, what podcasts do your potential customers listen to? Once you have narrowed down a list of podcasts, email them the undeniable reasons they should feature you on their podcast. Make this pitch short and poignant. Distinguish yourself as a leader in the industry and be very clear about why you will empower their audience. Add links to your website, press, and anything powerful that states that you are credible and a thought leader in this niche. Remember to make your contact information easily accessible so they can reach out with one click. Remember to make it brief.

<u>SEO/ Search Engine Optimizations-</u>are inextricably linked to brand visibility. The topic of **SEOs** is complex, yet so simple. Figure out what your potential client will type in a search engine to find your business. Once you have tapped into your future client's mind, use these keywords in all the content you produce. For example, smatter these keywords all over your website. Sprinkle them in your social media, in your press releases, and everything you send out into cyberspace.

VISIBILITY REVISITED

To start your brand-spanking-new business, you must create a vision for your brand and how you will represent this brand to the world is critical. Elevating this vision to capture the imagination of a targeted audience can be a labor of love. The visibility pillar will establish you in the game. Visibility is a consistent cadence of creatively thinking outside the box. Start small and do not give up.

<u>DO NOT GIVE UP!</u>

EVER!

The process of establishing a visible brand will distinguish you from your competitors. This process allows for trial and error, so dabble in different exercises of positioning your idea on various platforms. Remember, it takes time to start seeing results, but when you do, it is the sweetest validation of your hard work.

STOP CHASING YOUR DREAMS.

START BEING

SOCIAL MEDIA & DISEMPOWERMENT OF AN ILLUSION

Social media is a misunderstood spot in cyberspace. My experience on the biggies, Facebook and Instagram, has been an energy-sucking vortex of confusion and the addictive need to be liked and followed. I understand the draw to these powerful institutions. However, I stand firmly rooted in the fact that social media disempowers your marketing efforts. Social media is an illusion. This illusion is a carousel of momentary images that induce feelings of self-doubt and comparison. At an organic level, social media is a fabulous touch point to connect with long-lost friends. It allows you to share and catalog special moments. However, I feel strongly that social media is not the forum to sell your goods.

This, perhaps, is a confusing message. A common misconception about social media is that this is a platform to sell yourself. The truth is that the number of followers, likes, and heart emojis do not convert into sales. Social media is akin to marketing on borrowed land. You don't own this space, and you don't have any idea who sees your posts and when they see your posts. The social media algorithm, purposefully, remains a mystery. You do not have any control over your audience. The idea of borrowed-land in regards to social media means your marketing strategies are a crapshoot. Visibility is not guaranteed. What's more, your audience may not be specifically curated to your message. So, Filip, from Poland, may be the benefactor of all your female-inspired make-up tips.

The masterminds behind the powerhouses, Facebook and Instagram, have you believing that their tools will lead to success. These institutions have wielded a legend that the more followers you have, the more success you will receive.

BEWARE OF THE MYTH

FOLLOWERS=
INFLUENCE=
GUARANTEED SUCCESS

Followers = Influencer = Guaranteed Success

This line of thought can be rebutted by the fact that a mass following dilutes your message. Again, I emphasize that prioritizing your marketing efforts solely on social media is like marketing on borrowed land. When you have collected a large following, your audience spans many demographics, and many of these followers won't have an interest in your service or product. Coupled with this, the mysterious algorithms of Facebook and Instagram and the impact of your marketing strategies are left to the whims of the wizard behind the curtain.

If social media is a vortex of unpredictable exposure to a slightly interested audience, how can you firmly expand your visibility on solid ground?

Refer to the list above. Pique the interest of the audience who sits at the feet of your wisdom. And don't forget the almighty email list. The **email list** is the mightiest form of delivering impactful content to an audience who is already interested in you.

So, Why Use Social Media?

Admittedly, I have painted a negative image of social media. And the truth is, I have Facebook and Instagram accounts. These two polarizing stances don't seem to make sense at first. To clarify, social media is an excellent platform to establish visibility. Social media is an ideal platform to tell your story; however, it is not the place to sell.

Social media is a laser-focused tool for you to use in your business strategy—layer posts with gorgeous illustrations of what you do and what you love. **Instagram** is a place where you can send out a polished snapshot of your accomplishments. And **Facebook** is the perfect platform for you to engage future clients by hosting a group or a page. On Facebook, you can launch live broadcasts and speak on a soapbox. This allows you to create an authentic relationship with your audience and gain a sense of trust. Their curiosity will lead them to your website. And your website will illustrate your talents further. Ideally, your website will captivate this audience and transcend these users into devoted fans. Your website is where the magic happens.

IN CONCLUSION

I truly hope that you have received the core message of this workbook. You have the power to do anything you want. We are given such a brief time on this earth to live the life we are meant to live. So, this is the time to start believing in yourself. Your brilliant idea is worth so much more than you think. If you take action, your vision will be valuable and change lives.

Stay true to yourself and your vision. And never, ever give up. You got this.

Coach Jules

Hustle

Note from the Author

Stay True To Yourself, Stay True To Your Vision. Do not let self-doubt creep in and steer you in a direction that is deeply uncomfortable. Your success is dependent on staying authentic.

Notes & Take-Aways:

THE ULTIMATE GUIDE FOR NEW ENTREPRENUERS

HUSTLE SMART©

JULIE LOKUN

Facilitate Your Dreams. Learn How To Launch Your Idea Into A Thriving Business.